Corporate Marriage

Biblical Wisdom Combined with Business Strategies for a Marriage That Thrives

Kyle & Tomeka Speller

KSG Enterprises, LLC

Published by KSG Enterprises, LLC
www.KSG-Enterprises.com
1st Edition

ISBN: 979-8-9944426-09 (Paperback)
ISBN: 979-8-9944426-1-6 (Workbook)
ISBN: 979-8-9944426-2-3 (eBook)
Library of Congress Control Number: 2026901219
Authors' photos © by Tyler Speller

This publication includes or is inspired by design elements and graphics created using Canva. Such elements are used in accordance with Canva's free content license or under license from Canva. © Canva. No endorsement implied.

This book is intended for informational purposes only and does not guarantee specific outcomes. It is designed to support couples in pursuing healthy relationship goals, which the author and publisher make no guarantees of outcomes. It is also not a substitute for replacing any medical or psychological care, or legal advice. If you or someone you know is experiencing spousal or domestic abuse, seek immediate help from the National Domestic Violence Hotline at 1-800-799-7233. If you or your partner has been diagnosed with, or may be experiencing, a mental health condition, please seek professional assistance. The National Suicide & Crisis Lifeline is available 24/7 by dialing 988.

Printed in the United States of America.

Support for *Corporate Marriage*

"I remember my wedding day! So much anticipation and expectation for sharing the rest of my life with my college sweetheart. I wish we had Kyle and Tomeka's book to help us get started. Every marriage needs a vision, a purpose, a plan. This book is a "must read" for every marriage!"

~Donnie Dee, President/CEO
San Diego Rescue Mission

"In a world where marriages are often built on shifting sand, this book is a clarion call to return to the solid rock—God Himself—as the Head and Chief Executive of every covenant union. Rooted in timeless wisdom and the unchanging truth of the Book of Ephesians 5, it challenges couples to forsake worldly models and submit their homes wholly unto the Lord. If ye seek a marriage where Christ leads, love abounds, and purpose is fulfilled, then this book is a divine blueprint. Let God be your CEO, and thy house shall surely stand." Then you will build a healthy happy and Holy family with the help of the Holy Spirit. - Pray Now"

~Pastor Alvin Simpkins, Phd
Senior Pastor Emmanuel Christian Center – Aurora, CO

"This book is an uplifting and invaluable resource for any couple seeking to build a stronger, God-centered marriage. The Spellers have provided biblical wisdom and practical guidance, emphasizing the transformative power of placing Christ at the heart of your union. Through insightful teachings and relatable examples, this book will encourage you to cultivate a deeper love and commitment, fostering a partnership that thrives on faith, communication, and mutual respect. It's a wonderful guide for both newly engaged couples and those celebrating many years together, offering a refreshing perspective on navigating the joys and challenges of marriage God's way."

~Gerald Albright
9-time Grammy Nominated Recording
Saxophonist & Musician

Book Dedication

Dear Tyler, Christian, and Christopher,

We dedicate this book to you.

You are now adults, each walking your own unique path, and it has been one of our greatest joys to witness the lives you are building. We are incredibly proud of who you are and who you continue to become.

We have been enormously blessed to be your parents. We have done our best to raise you in the ways of our Lord and Savior, knowing full well that we are far from perfect. Along the way, you have taught us just as much as we have tried to teach you—about life, grace, compassion, love, and sacrifice. For that, we are deeply grateful.

Tyler, thank you for showing us what it truly means to have a servant's heart and a spirit of genuine care for others.

Christian, thank you for reminding us to keep our sense of humor while pursuing ambition and purpose.

Christopher, thank you for teaching us the power of self-discipline, loyalty, and kindness.

We love you all—always and forever. There's greatness inside of you!

With all our love,
Dad and Mom

Contents

Foreword

I met Kyle and Tomeka at different times in life, but over the years, I've come to know them both well—and deeply respect the strength of their character and the integrity of their journey.

Kyle played a meaningful role in one of the most special moments of my life: he officiated the vow renewal ceremony for my wife and me on our 10th anniversary. That same sense of care and presence he brought to our celebration, I've seen him bring to many others—officiating weddings for close friends and family and always showing up as a man of steady faith and heartfelt leadership.

Together, Kyle and Tomeka are rooted in their love for family. Knowing them, it comes as no surprise that they've come together to write a book aimed at uplifting couples and families. This isn't just another relationship book—it's a reflection of their lived values, hard-earned wisdom, and the intentional life they've built together.

The life of a professional athlete, head coach, and businessman is anything but ordinary. It demands focus, sacrifice, and an unshakable foundation of faith. That same energy—the dedication, purpose, and resilience—is what Corporate Marriage offers to readers.

As a young husband and father, I leaned on voices that inspired me—people who didn't just offer advice but lived out the kind of marriage I aspired to, which I am blessed to have today. People who showed up with encouragement, truth, and love. That's exactly what Kyle and Tomeka offer in these pages: practical, honest, and uplifting guidance you can rely on—whether you're dating, engaged, or have been married for decades.

This book will be a tool you can pull out in the sunny seasons of love and through the challenging winter months. I stand behind the strategies and the hearts of the authors.

~Chauncey Billups
Family Man &
2004 NBA Champion & Finals MVP
5x NBA All-Star, 3x All-NBA,
NBA Hall Of Famer

A Note from the Authors

Dear Readers,

Corporate Marriage and its accompanying workbook (sold separately) will not be for every couple. However, it is our heart's desire that this work would be a blessing to those who have chosen to take this journey with us.

Even more importantly, you have likely chosen to take this journey alongside your spouse, and it is our sincere prayer that your union will be drawn closer together through God's Living Word and the vision He has given us through this resource.

Romans 8:1 reminds us that there is *no condemnation* for those who are in Christ Jesus. We are all a work in progress—continually being sanctified as we walk with the Lord. Wherever you may be on your life's journey, know that grace meets you there.

As you move through these pages, we invite you to open your hearts and allow the Holy Spirit to speak, to heal, and to grow the marriage union God created you to enjoy. May He strengthen your relationship as a reflection of the sacred marriage between Christ and His Church.

Our encouragement to you: Lean in fully. Be honest. Be prayerful. Commit to the process together, trusting God with both the beautiful and the broken places. Allow Him to do what only He can do.

God bless you as you begin this journey. May your marriage be renewed, restored, and rooted deeply in His love.

Introduction

You don't need another marriage book filled with fluff, formulas, or false promises. You need something real. Grounded. Strategic. Biblical - **with God as CEO.**

If you're like most people, you've been taught how to succeed in the marketplace—how to plan, lead, build, and grow. You know how to set goals, manage projects, and drive results. But when it comes to marriage? Most of us were never trained to win at home.

We chase success at work but feel stuck at the dinner table. We lead meetings with excellence but struggle to lead with love. We manage teams with precision but can't seem to manage tension with our spouse. Why?

Because we've separated what God never meant to be divided: **purpose and partnership, vision and intimacy, strategy and covenant**.

This book is built on a simple but powerful truth: **Marriage is not just a relationship—it's a divine mission.**

It deserves more than good intentions.

It needs a **plan**.

Just like any successful business or ministry, a thriving marriage must be built with clarity, discipline, and grace. You need vision for where you're going. Systems that keep love alive. Values that shape your decisions. Metrics that keep you accountable. And, most of all, **faith that fuels every step**.

Throughout this book, we'll explore what it means to lead and love with purpose. We'll unpack real principles—from both Scripture and strategy—that will help you and your spouse build something lasting. Not perfect. Not easy. But intentional, Spirit-led, and deeply rewarding.

Whether you're newly married or decades in, whether you're thriving or just trying to survive—this is your invitation.

To pause.

To reflect.
To recalibrate.

To build your marriage with the same care and conviction you give to every other area of purpose in your life.

Because when your marriage is in alignment with God's design, it doesn't just bless your home—it impacts generations.

Corporate Marriage draws a powerful parallel between two institutions that demand structure, strategy, and sacrifice: business and marriage.

Many people know how to show up professionally—meeting deadlines, building systems, leading teams—but often neglect the same level of intentionality and excellence at home.

This book challenges husbands and wives to apply *corporate-level principles* to the most sacred partnership of all: **marriage**.

Just like successful companies thrive with:

- Clear **vision**
- Servant **leadership**
- Efficient **communication**
- Strategic **planning**
- Measurable **goals**
- Culture-building **values**

...so too can a marriage grow stronger, deeper, and more fruitful.

Biblical Foundation – Ephesians 5:21–33

Ephesians 5 reminds us that marriage is not just a social contract—it's a **spiritual covenant** designed by God. It reflects the relationship between **Christ and the Church**. Within this divine blueprint, we find:

- **Mutual submission** (v.21)

- **Servant leadership** (v.25)

- **Respect and reverence** (v.33)

- **Spiritual purpose and alignment**

Corporate Marriage brings this sacred text into modern language, helping readers **organize** their marriages with purpose, passion, and faith.

Let's build—together.

1

Begin with the End in Mind

Building a Marriage That Lasts

Managing relationships is tough in today's world.

We live in a culture of instant gratification and disposable commitments. Whether it's friendships, business partnerships, or marriages, there's often more emphasis on short-term feelings than long-term faithfulness. But if we want to succeed in marriage—truly succeed—we must begin with the end in mind.

In business, no successful company is built by accident. Behind every thriving brand is a clear **vision**, a determined **plan**, and the willingness to put in consistent **work**. It's no different in marriage.

Vision: The Why Behind the Work

Vision gives you direction. It tells you **why** you're doing what you're doing. Without vision, the marriage can begin to drift—just like a business without purpose eventually crumbles.

Proverbs 29:18 says, *"Where there is no vision, the people perish."* The same is true of couples—where there is no shared vision, the relationship begins to decay. Studies show that up to 70% of marriages fail when couples have no clear direction, no shared goals, and no unified purpose.

A healthy marriage asks questions like:

- What do we want our relationship to look like 10 years from now?
- What kind of home environment do we want to create?
- How do we want to raise our children?
- What legacy do we want to leave?

Without a vision, you're just reacting. But with vision, you can respond with purpose.

Blueprint: Building Something That Will Last

It's not enough to dream big—you have to **build wisely**.

A blueprint is defined as "a detailed plan or program of action." Every lasting marriage is built on more than feelings and chemistry. It's built on intention, wisdom, and commitment.

Let's break it down:

- **The Foundation:**
  Every structure needs a solid base. For a Christian marriage, that foundation must be Christ. Matthew 7:24-25 talks about the wise man who built his house on the rock—when the storms came, the house stood firm. Your foundation determines your stability in the storms.

- **The Materials:**
  Are you building your marriage with **cheap substitutes**—like pride, selfishness, or emotional withdrawal? Or are you using **quality materials** like love, patience, humility, and grace?

- **The Hours of Labor:**
  Every great marriage requires **intentional effort**. You can't just put in work when it's convenient. Are you slacking off emotionally, spiritually, or relationally? Or are you showing up, even when it's hard?

- **Recognizing the Seasons:**
  Just like in construction, timing matters. There's a time to lay sod and a time to let it grow. In marriage, there are seasons of planting, growing, pruning, and harvesting. Can you recognize what season your marriage is in? Are you being patient during the winter seasons, and sowing during the spring?

- **Curb Appeal vs. Structural Integrity:**
  Some marriages look good from the outside but are falling apart within. God doesn't just care about how

your relationship **looks**—He cares about how it's **built**. Don't be content with appearances. Build with integrity.

Adaptability and Innovation

Just like businesses need to evolve to stay relevant, marriages must **grow** and **adapt**.

That doesn't mean compromising your values—it means being sensitive to the changing dynamics of life. Careers shift. Children grow. Personal needs and desires develop over time. The couples who survive and thrive are those who are **flexible**, **innovative**, and **willing to grow** together.

Stagnation leads to frustration. But growth—when done together—leads to deeper connection.

Have a Plan

At the end of the day, no vision will work unless you put it into action. You can dream about a great marriage, but if you don't have a plan, you'll keep repeating the same mistakes.

What's your **strategy** for:

- Communicating effectively?
- Resolving conflict?
- Prioritizing intimacy?
- Nurturing spiritual health?

A great marriage doesn't happen by chance—it's **designed**, **built**, and **maintained** over time.

Developing Your Marriage Plan – The Business of Building Love

Every strong business has a business plan. Without one, it drifts into confusion, chaos, and eventual collapse. Likewise, every strong **marriage** needs a **Marriage Plan**—a clear strategy that defines roles, expectations, vision, and methods of growth.

Let's explore 8 core categories found in a business plan, and how they directly apply to the health of your marriage.

1. **Corporate Governance – Leading with Love**
2. **Environmental Analysis – Knowing Your Climate**
3. **Human Capital Strategy – Investing in Each Other**
4. **Marketing – Communicating Value**
5. **Statistics – Measuring What Matters**
6. **Financial Analysis – Stewarding Your Resources**
7. **Project Management – Working Toward Shared Dreams**
8. **Operations Management – Daily Habits That Sustain Love**

2

Corporate Governance
Leading with Love

Everything rises and falls on **leadership**—and in the marriage context, both spouses lead. Healthy marriages are led by mutual **service, respect**, and **spiritual guidance**.

"But he that is greatest among you shall be your servant."
— Matthew 23:11

Leadership Lessons for Marriage:

Tip

- **Stay Hungry**
  Satisfaction can be a silent killer. When you get too comfortable, you stop pursuing each other.

- **Keep dating your spouse.** Keep complimenting. Keep romancing. Don't lose your "rap" (smooth lines you used to get each other).

- **Avoid the Holding Pattern**
  Like a plane circling the runway, you might be moving but going nowhere. Break the cycles—drop the weight, confess the sin, and move forward in faith.

    Hebrews 12:1 — "Let us lay aside every weight… and let us run with patience the race that is set before us,"

- **Reject Complacency**
  Shortcuts in marriage lead to long-term damage. If you want something meaningful, you'll have to **work for it**.

- **Have a Plan**
  Failing to plan is planning to fail. Talk often about your goals—financial, spiritual, and emotional. Pray over your direction together.

- **Master Your Emotions**
  Anger left unchecked will destroy intimacy. Pray before you react.

  > *James 1:19 — "be swift to hear, slow to speak, slow to wrath:"*

- **Guard Your Tongue**
  Words can build or destroy. Speak **life**, not curses. Call out greatness in your spouse—even when you don't feel like it.

  > *Proverbs 18:21 — "Death and life are in the power of the tongue."*

Handling Conflict: Practical Tools for Peace

Here are **9 ways to restore joy** when your spouse is unhappy:

1. **Hear them out** – Don't interrupt or try to fix it immediately.

2. **Show regret** – "I'm sorry this happened…" goes a long way.

3. **Lead with empathy** – Validate their feelings without comparing stories.

4. **Investigate** – Ask deeper questions to understand the root, not just the symptoms.

5. **Clarify what they want** – You can't hit a target you don't see.

6. **Be honest about your capacity** – Say what you *can* and *can't* do.

7. **Make a plan together**

8. **Follow through**

9. **Check back** – Restoration needs follow-up.

10 Simple Phrases That Diffuse Tension

Sometimes the right words cool the flame:

1. Please
2. Thank you
3. I'm sorry
4. Excuse me
5. You're welcome
6. I'm sorry to keep you waiting
7. Thank you for waiting
8. Is there anything else I can do for you?
9. I appreciate you
10. May I help you?

 The Final Word: This Marriage Needs God

You cannot lead well, serve well, or grow well without **God's help**. Don't rely on your own strength.

Psalm 46:1 — "God is our refuge and strength, a very present help in trouble."

Ask the Lord daily for:

- **Illumination** – God's insight when things are unclear.
- **Strength** – For days when emotions and exhaustion try to take over.
- **Stretching** – So you don't stay stuck where you are.

If you don't stretch with God, the enemy will stretch you in ways that hurt. **Let God lead**—and let your plan be led by **faith, not just formulas**.

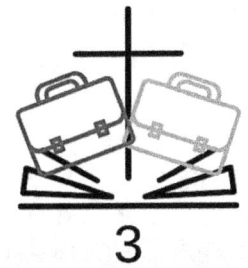

3

Environmental Analysis
Understanding the Changing Landscape of Marriage

Every successful business regularly conducts an **environmental analysis**—a deep look at the changing conditions around and within the organization. Why? Because the environment is **never static**. The moment you stop paying attention to what's changing is the moment you start falling behind.

Marriage works the same way. The cultural climate, your personal responsibilities, your emotions, and even your spiritual walk are all subject to **change and growth**. The goal of this chapter is to help couples recognize and respond wisely to those changes—together.

In business, environmental analysis assesses market trends and competition. In marriage, it's about recognizing the **external and internal factors** that influence your relationship.

Ask questions such as:

- What season are we in? (Newlyweds, parenting, empty nest?)

- Are there stressors affecting our intimacy?

- What outside voices (media, friends, culture) are shaping our values?

A good marriage responds to its environment with **discernment**, not panic.

4 Seasons in Marriage:

Your relationship does not exist in a vacuum. It is constantly shaped by:

- Career demands
- Parenting responsibilities
- Health changes

- Emotional wounds
- Spiritual growth (or stagnation)
- Cultural pressure
- Time

Ignoring these forces doesn't make them go away—it just leaves you unprepared.

One of the most helpful ways to understand the changing landscape of marriage is through recognizing **seasons**. Just as nature moves through predictable cycles, marriages do too.

"To everything there is a season, and a time to every purpose under the heaven:" — Ecclesiastes 3:1

Seasons are not failures.
They are signals.

When couples misinterpret seasons, they panic, blame, or quit.
When they understand seasons, they adjust, endure, and grow.

Let's examine the **4 seasons of marriage**.

WINTER: When Love Feels Cold, Distant, and Dormant

Winter in marriage symbolizes **emotional coldness, hardship, and disconnection**. It is often the most misunderstood—and most feared—season.

In winter, couples may feel like they are "Living beside one another, but not in union with one another."

This season can include:

- Emotional distance
- Reduced communication
- Unresolved conflict
- Bitterness or disappointment

- Loneliness—even while sharing the same bed

Winter feels quiet, heavy, and exhausting. But winter is not the end. It is a **dormant season**, not a dead one.

Just as plants pull inward to survive harsh conditions, marriages sometimes hibernate—not to die, but to endure.

Signs You May Be in a Winter Season

- Conversations feel transactional or surface-level
- Physical affection decreases
- You feel misunderstood or unseen
- You're more roommates than partners
- Resentment simmers beneath the surface

Winter often isn't caused by a single event—it's usually the result of **life pressure**.

What a Colder Season Might Look Like

- Demanding jobs or business travel
- Heavy workloads and mental fatigue
- Extreme focus on children (sports, practices, doctor appointments)
- Financial stress
- Health challenges
- Emotional burnout

None of these things are "bad." But when left unchecked, they become **barriers to connection**.

If you don't identify the barriers, distance becomes normalized—and intimacy slowly erodes.

Making the Best of a Winter Season

Winter requires **intentional warmth**.

- Recommit to **date nights**, even simple ones
- Watch a winter movie together (yes—even cheesy/same storyline Christmas movies ☺)
- Cook a warm meal together
- Pray intentionally *for* your spouse, not *about* them.
    - When you pray for your spouse, the Holy Spirit reshapes and transforms your heart to reflect God's heart toward them. Prayer also invites the Holy Spirit to replace frustration with compassion and aligns your heart with God's heart for your spouse. The Holy Spirit will also give you God's perspective—and His heart—toward the one you love.
- Ask God: *"Show me how to love my spouse in this season."*
- Practice physical affection **without a sexual agenda**—hugs, holding hands, sitting close

Why does this matter?

Because many couples forget **how to be together at home—**the very place intimacy matters most.

Winter is where vows are tested:

"For better or for worse."

Faithfulness in winter builds the trust needed for spring.

SPRING: New Beginnings, Hope, and Fresh Growth

Spring represents **renewal**.

This may come after a hard season, or it may arrive unexpectedly. Communication improves. Hope returns. Laughter feels easier. Emotional walls begin to soften.

Spring reminds couples Love can grow again.

But spring is fragile.

What grows depends entirely on **what you plant**.

"Be not deceived; God is not mocked: for whatsoever a man [sows], that shall he also reap." — *Galatians 6:7*

What a Time of Planting Might Look Like

- Reassessing each other's needs (they change over time)
- Reading a relationship or marriage book together
- Renewed spiritual connection
- New goals or dreams emerging

Never stop planting.
Never stop learning your spouse.

You will **never fully master** your spouse. There are layers of their heart, history, and personality that may not surface until later seasons of life.

Some places in the heart lie dormant until the right time.

Making the Best of a Spring Season

- Leave winter behind—don't rehearse old pain
- Embrace change with optimism
- Be gentle and kind
- Build positive goals together
    - Financial goals
    - Travel plans
    - Spiritual rhythms
- Address difficult topics with grace and clarity
- Be intentional about the **crop** you're planting

Spring is often the right time for:

- Forgiveness

- Apologies
- Fresh starts

"…Write the vision and make it plain…" — *Habakkuk 2:2*

When God brings you into spring, **don't waste it**. Grow.

SUMMER: Passion, Connection, and Shared Joy

Summer represents the **peak season**—when marriage feels joyful, connected, and fulfilling.

Communication flows.
Affection is natural.
Laughter is frequent.
Life feels lighter.

This is the season couples often assume will last forever.

But summer carries a quiet danger: **complacency**.

What Summer Might Look Like

- Relaxed rhythm
- Adventure and fun
- Minimal conflict
- Emotional safety
- You've recently overcome a hard season

This is the season to **build reserves**.

Just like businesses prepare for downturns during profitable seasons, marriages must store emotional capital while things are good.

Making the Best of a Summer Season

- Practice gratitude daily
- Enjoy rest together

- Create meaningful memories
- Say "no" to unnecessary demands
- Protect margin

"[There is] a time to heal…" — *Ecclesiastes 3:3*

Store joy. Store trust. Store affection.

What you build in summer will carry you through winter.

FALL: Transition, Tension, and Warning Signs

Fall is the **transition season**—often subtle, but significant.

The temperature shifts.
Small irritations feel bigger.
Patience shortens.
Communication becomes strained.

Fall is not yet winter—but it's a warning.

What Fall Might Look Like

- Feeling easily annoyed
- Reduced patience
- Shrugging off your spouse's needs
- Less energy to talk things through
- Emotional fatigue

If ignored, fall becomes winter.

Making the Best of a Fall Season

- Be adaptable and flexible
- Create space for rest and reflection (not emotional distance)
- Revisit a list of things you love and appreciate about your spouse
- Address issues early—before resentment takes root

Fall is a **course-correction season**.

Wise couples slow down here instead of pushing through blindly.

Learning the Seasons Together

Over time, couples learn how to **move through seasons faster and healthier** than they did early in marriage. Why?

Because marriage is no longer about *just you*.

It becomes:

- Shared life
- Shared responsibility
- Shared growth

Marriage is not about having your needs met alone. It's about building a life together.

When couples understand seasons, they stop asking: "What's wrong with us?"

And start asking: "What does this season require from us?"

That shift changes everything.

Key Truth to Remember

Seasons change—but covenant remains.

Learn the landscape.
Adjust your strategy.
Stay committed.

Spring always comes.

Cultural Change: Recognizing the Shifts Around You

Ecclesiastes 3:1 — "To every thing there is a season, and a time to every purpose under heaven:"

In every generation, culture changes—and it's changing **faster than ever**. Technology, gender roles, social values, family structures, and even the expectations people place on marriage all shift over time. If we don't pay attention, we can end up building our marriage around outdated assumptions or harmful trends.

Examples of Cultural Changes That Affect Marriage:

- **Technology:** Increased screen time affects communication and intimacy.

- **Career Demands:** Longer work hours and dual-income households impact family rhythms.

- **Parenting Styles:** Shifting values about discipline, education, and screen time can divide couples.

- **Cultural Pressures:** Society often values individualism over sacrifice, self-expression over humility, and instant gratification over commitment—all of which run counter to biblical marriage.

We're called to **watch over the ways of our household**, not just react to whatever is trending.

Proverbs 31:27 — "She [looks] well to the ways of her household, and [eats] not the bread of idleness."

This verse highlights the importance of vigilance, awareness, and **proactive care**. As a couple, you're the **watchmen** over your home. Pay attention to what's influencing your family—and make sure it aligns with God's vision.

Organizational Behavior: Understanding Patterns in Your Relationship

In business, **organizational behavior** refers to the patterns, roles, and dynamics within a company. In marriage, it's about how **you and your spouse function together**—your habits, communication styles, conflict patterns, and emotional rhythms.

Start by asking:

- What patterns are we repeating—healthy or unhealthy?

- Are we working as a **team**, or drifting into **individual lanes**?

- Do we understand and respect each other's roles?

Understanding Roles in Marriage:

This isn't about strict gender stereotypes — it's about **function** and **flow**. Every couple should take time to identify:

- Who leads in spiritual decisions?

- Who manages finances?

- Who coordinates the household or parenting logistics?

- Who supports emotional and spiritual needs?

These roles **evolve** through seasons. What worked when you were newlyweds may not work during parenthood. Communication and **adaptability** are essential.

Amos 3:3 — "Can two walk together, except they be agreed?"

Alignment in your roles brings peace. Confusion creates chaos.

SWOTT Analysis: A Strategic Look at Your Marriage

In business, a **SWOTT Analysis** helps leaders assess internal and external factors that impact success. It's a powerful tool in marriage as well. Here's how to break it down:

S – Strengths (Internal Positives)

- What are the strengths of your relationship?
- What makes you unique as a couple?
- What has helped you endure hard times?

➡ *List the top 3 strengths you bring to the relationship.*

Examples: Shared faith, open communication, sense of humor, unity in parenting.

W – Weaknesses (Internal Challenges)

- Where do you consistently struggle?
- What unresolved patterns keep resurfacing?
- Are there past hurts that still influence your interactions?

➡ *Identify areas where you need grace and growth.*

Examples: Poor communication under stress, financial disorganization, lack of emotional intimacy.

O – Opportunities (External Possibilities)

- What could you do together that strengthens your future?
- Are there mentors or ministries you can connect with?
- Could a season of change (new job, move, etc.) become a launching pad?

➡ *Recognize where God might be calling you to grow or serve.*

Examples: Joining a marriage group, starting a family devotional, traveling together to reconnect.

T – Threats (External Pressures or Risks)

- What outside influences are affecting your relationship?

- Are there people or habits pulling you apart?

- Is work, social media, or entertainment stealing quality time?

➡️ *Be honest and name the threats—so you can fight them together.*

Examples: Flirting at work, extended family drama, screen addiction, comparison via social media.

T – Trends (Ongoing Shifts to Watch)

- What trends are forming in your marriage or home?

- Are you growing closer or drifting apart?

- Are there spiritual patterns—positive or negative—taking shape?

➡️ *Pay attention to small shifts before they become big problems—or missed blessings.*

Examples: Growing resentment, spiritual laziness, increased laughter, stronger communication.

 ## Conclusion: Stay Watchful. Stay Willing. Stay in Step.

Environmental analysis isn't a one-time event—it's a lifestyle of **awareness and responsiveness**. God calls us to **watch**, to **steward**, and to **respond with wisdom** to the changes in our lives and homes. Seasons will come and go. Roles will shift. Circumstances will evolve. But a couple who stays **attuned to the environment** and **anchored in Christ** will thrive in every season.

Isaiah 43:19 — "Behold, I will do a new thing; now it shall spring forth; shall you not know it?"

Don't fear change. Embrace it—with God, with grace, and with each other.

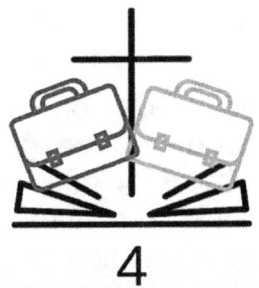

4

Human Capital
Strategy

Every thriving business knows that its **greatest asset is its people**—its "human capital." The same is true in marriage. Your most important investment isn't the house, the money, or the accomplishments. It's each other.

To build a high-performing, God-honoring marriage, you need a **strategy for connection, service, growth, and longevity**. This chapter outlines what it looks like to intentionally invest in your spouse—not just emotionally or physically, but spiritually, mentally, and relationally.

In business, human capital refers to the people who make the company thrive. In marriage, it's **you and your spouse**—your time, energy, growth, and effort.

Strategies for marital investment:

- **Pray together.** Couples that pray together, stay together.

- **Pursue personal growth.** A growing individual makes for a thriving spouse.

- **Create shared goals.** Don't just live under the same roof—live under the same mission.

Intimacy – "In-to-me-see"

Let's start with a key part of human capital: **connection**. Intimacy isn't just about sex. It's about **knowing and being known**, seeing and being seen, and creating a **safe space** where vulnerability is welcomed and valued.

Genesis 2:25 — "And they were both naked, the man and his wife, and were not ashamed."

That's more than physical. That's full transparency and trust.

What intimacy looks like:

- Honest conversations without fear of judgment

- Affection without performance pressure

- Spiritual connection through prayer and shared faith

- Making time to connect even when life is busy

Men are usually like **microwaves**—ready in 30 seconds.

Women tend to be more like **crock pots**—they need warmth, time, attention, and emotional safety.

The goal isn't just to **get intimacy**, but to **give it**. True intimacy asks: "Do you feel seen, heard, and loved today?"

"Doin' Some Connecting":

- Touch base emotionally every day. (How are you? What's on your mind?)

- Learn to read your spouse's emotional temperature.

- Make room for date nights, cuddles, and undistracted conversation.

- Flirt again. Laugh again. Play again. Pursue each other.

Marriage Relations = Customer Service

In the business world, service is about **meeting and anticipating the needs** of customers. In marriage, **you are each other's number one customer.** Your job is to serve—not selfishly consume, and **you'll never go wrong trying to out serve each other.**

Philippians 2:3 — "Let nothing be done through strife or vainglory; but in lowliness of mind let each esteem other better than themselves."

Redefining Service in Marriage:

- **Anticipate needs**—not just react to complaints.

- **Commit to understanding** what makes your spouse feel loved, secure, and appreciated.

- **Listen to serve, not to win.**

High-performing marriages excel because they approach service like a calling, not a chore.

Keys to Effective Service:

- Listen actively: Understand → Clarify → Offer solutions → Follow up

- View adversity as opportunity—not a threat.

- Don't ration love based on what your spouse did or didn't do. ("I'm not doing that because they didn't…") The love of Jesus doesn't say I love you if you love me – it simply says I love you.

Great marriages are built by spouses who are committed to **out-serving each other**.

High-Performing Couples Do These Things Well:

Let's break it down into three performance categories: **Character**, **Contribution**, and **Connection**.

1. Character: Respect, Interdependency, Reciprocity

Ecclesiastes 4:9–10 — "Two are better than one… For if they fall, the one will lift up his fellow:…"

How to build it:

- Support your spouse's success. (emotionally, professionally, spiritually)

- Keep promises. Don't erode trust with broken words.
- Embrace each other's differences—see your diversity as an advantage, not a problem.
- Practice **recognition**: say "thank you" often, celebrate effort and progress.
- Carry your share of the load—no freeloaders in marriage.
- See each other the way **God sees you**—as sons and daughters of the King.

2. Contribution: Focus, Dedication, Collaboration

Amos 3:3 — "Can two walk together, except they be agreed?"

How to build it:

- Refocus on shared goals daily. (spiritual, financial, emotional, family)
- Speak up instead of bottling things in.
- Pursue the right solutions, not just your own preferences.
- If it needs to be done—**do it now.** (Don't wait until it's a problem)
- Celebrate every win—big or small. Joy keeps you resilient.

The enemy will constantly whisper what you're **not**. You must remind each other what you **are**—loved, chosen, growing, and together.

3. Connection: Communication, Trust, Safety

Ephesians 4:15 — "Speaking the truth in love..."

How to build it:

- Go to the source: Don't gossip about your spouse to others. Go directly to them.

- Attack the problem—not the person. (*Ephesians 6:12* — *"We wrestle not against flesh and blood..."*)
- Accept responsibility and avoid the blame game.
- Address issues early, before they fester.
- Assume the best about each other's intentions.

(We judge ourselves by our intentions, but others by their actions—be fair.)

James 1:19 — "...let every man be swift to hear, slow to speak, slow to wrath:"

 ## Conclusion: Marriage as a Stewardship of People

Just like a wise CEO cares deeply about the health of their team, you are called to **care deeply and intentionally** about your spouse. Marriage is not about perfect performance—it's about faithful stewardship.

Let your **strategy** be based on God's design:

- Serve each other humbly.

- Build intimacy through consistent connection.

- Communicate with honesty and grace.

- Work together like a high-performing team.

Colossians 3:23 — "And whatsoever [you] do, do it heartily, as to the Lord, and not unto men;"

You're not just building a marriage. You're building a **legacy**. One full of love, growth, and God's glory.

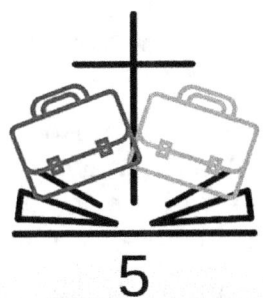

5

Marketing
How You Show Up in Your Marriage

In business, **marketing is how you present your product to the world**. It's the image, the tone, the message, the promise—and whether or not you consistently **deliver on what you advertised**.

In marriage, **your brand is YOU**. And let's be honest: some of us advertised ourselves one way during the "courtship campaign," but once we got the "contract signed" (wedding vows), we let the brand go stale.

If we want to have a high-performing, healthy marriage, we must become intentional about **how we show up** to each other—daily. Great marketing attracts, builds trust, and communicates value. Weak marketing? It misleads, frustrates, and causes confusion.

Marketing in business is about showing the world your value. In marriage, it's about continually **communicating your love** and **reaffirming your commitment**.

Ask: What message am I sending my spouse every day?

Sometimes we communicate more by what we don't say. Your tone, facial expressions, appreciation, and affirmation all matter.

Don't Get Stuck in Regressed Development

Remember when you first met? You put in WORK.

- You dressed to impress.
- You texted "good morning" and "goodnight."
- You planned dates.
- You talked for hours. ("You hang up first… No you hang up first…")
- You made her feel *seen*, *heard*, and *wanted.*

Now? You're wearing the same holey t-shirt from 2010 and calling it loungewear. You went from Barry White to barely right. 😄

You got the job—but are you still producing?

Marriage isn't a finish line—it's a **growth line**. If your pursuit stopped at the wedding altar, you didn't marry a wife—you secured a transaction. But if you want passion, friendship, and joy to stay alive, you must **keep marketing who you are becoming**.

Leveling Up the Presentation

Men:

When you were dating, you spared no expense—flowers, cologne, fresh haircuts. But now? You are arguing about going to Bath & Body Works or upgrading your wife's Moo Moo.

Brothers—**invest in her like you did when you were trying to get her**. That doesn't just mean money—it means **energy, compliments, attention, quality time**. It means:

- Planning surprises

- Giving her something new to smile about

- Learning what her "love language" is and speaking it fluently

Ladies:

Your man doesn't need perfection—but he still wants pursuit. He needs admiration, attention, softness, joy.

That "Victoria's Secret Moo Moo"? That's not just about clothing—it's about **intention**. About reminding your husband he's still the man you prayed for, and he's still got it.

I *Corporate Marriage:* Kyle & Tomeka Speller I

Marketing in marriage means you don't just present your best self in public—but even more so in private.

Keep Your Honey on Your Mind

Let your marriage be one where:

- **Affection isn't rationed**

- **Passion isn't buried under the laundry pile**

- You're not roommates, co-parents, or business partners—but **lovers and friends** on purpose

Trust: Trust Each Other Like You're on the Same Team

Trust is the currency of every strong brand—and every strong marriage. If your words and actions don't align, your spouse will **stop believing the advertisement**.

Matthew 5:37 — "But let your communication be, [Yes, yes; No, no]:"

- Build trust through **consistency.**

- Keep your word—even in small things.

- Apologize quickly and forgive freely.

- Be **safe** emotionally and spiritually.

Communication: Don't Talk to Each Other Any Old Kind of Way

Galatians 5:22-23 — "But the fruit of the Spirit is love, joy, peace, longsuffering, gentleness, goodness, faith, meekness, temperance:..."

These are the **filters** for communication in marriage.

Let's be real: most arguments aren't about what was said—but **how it was said**.

When you communicate:

- **Tone matters**
- **Timing matters**
- **Non-verbal signals matter**
- **Empathy matters**

The hallmark of a great team is not the absence of conflict. It's the maturity to handle it well.

Put the cause before self. It's not about winning the fight—it's about building the future.

Non-Verbal Communication: You're Always Saying Something

We often think communication is just **words**—but research says otherwise:

Type	Percentage
Verbal (words)	7%
Vocal (tone of voice)	38%
Visual (body language)	55%

Non-verbal communication carries 8x the impact of your words.

That means:

- Your eye-rolls speak louder than your "I'm fine."
- Your silence can feel like punishment.

- Your posture, face, and touch (or lack thereof) are all broadcasting messages.

Eye Contact: Connection in the First 10 Seconds

Studies show:

- Eye contact **60–80%** **of** **the** **time** = reliable, trustworthy, connected

- Eye contact **30–40% of the time** = distant, suspicious, disengaged

Look your spouse in the eyes. Really see them. It communicates: *"I'm present. You matter. I care."*

Body Language & Gestures

Posture says a lot:

- Lean in = I'm interested

- Arms crossed = I'm closed off

- Facing your spouse directly = I'm engaged

- Angled away = I'm detached

Gestures to Watch:

- Frowning, sighing, biting lips in frustration

- Texting or scrolling while they're talking

- Physical distancing during conflict

These all say: *"I don't value this moment."* But that's not who you are. You're building something sacred.

Facial Expressions & Smiling

Proverbs 15:13 — "A merry heart [makes] a cheerful countenance..."

How often do you smile at each other?

A smile is:

- A **connection point**
- A **barrier breaker**
- A small act that creates a **safe space**

Even if things are hard, your face can still say: *"We're in this together. I'm still glad I chose you."*

 Summary: Make Your Marriage Irresistible Again

You don't need to be a marketing genius to build a beautiful marriage. You just need to:

- **Be intentional** about how you show up.
- **Invest in your spouse's joy.**
- **Communicate with kindness.**
- **Let your non-verbal language match your love.**
- **Trust each other like you're on the same team.** (Because you are!)

Proverbs 3:3–4 — "Let not mercy and truth forsake [you]:... So [shall you] find favor and good understanding in the sight of God and man."

Let your marriage be **your best campaign**. A story that sells hope. A love that doesn't just say "I do" once—but says it **every day**.

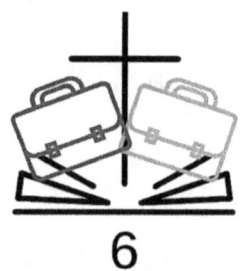

6

Statistics
What the Numbers Are Saying

You don't need to be a data analyst to understand that **patterns, probabilities, and principles** matter in life—and especially in marriage. Whether in business or relationships, statistics help us interpret what's likely to happen based on consistent inputs, actions, or behaviors.

In your marriage, you are gathering data every day—even if you don't realize it. **The words you speak. The habits you build. The prayers you pray. The time you give. The attitude you bring.** All of it forms a pattern that predicts your future.

So, let's get into some **relationship statistics**—and why they matter in your home.

Good businesses measure performance. Strong marriages do, too. Not everything needs a spreadsheet, but you should regularly evaluate:

- Are we praying together?

- When was our last date night?

- Are we resolving conflict or avoiding it?

- Is our intimacy growing?

Track **what matters**, and you'll start to improve what matters.

Probability Concepts – Recognizing Patterns That Predict Outcomes

Probability is the measure of how likely something is to happen. It doesn't guarantee the future—but it gives you a high-level view of what your actions are trending toward.

"[You] shall know them by their fruits..." –Matthew 7:16

Here are a few spiritual probability truths worth remembering:

- **Statistically speaking, if you don't PRAY, you will become PREY.**

- o A prayerless marriage is a vulnerable marriage.
- o "Your adversary the devil, as a roaring lion, [walks] about, seeking whom he may devour:" – 1 Peter 5:8 — and divided, distracted, prayerless couples are his easiest targets.

- **Couples who PRAY together tend to STAY together.**
  - o Prayer fosters unity, healing, and humility.
  - o It brings God into the middle of your mess—and that's always a game-changer.

- **Couples who PLAY together stay together.**
  - o Laughter, recreation, shared joy—these are **emotional glues.**
  - o Don't just share bills. Share jokes, dreams, and fun.

- **Couples who focus on GOD grow closer to each other.**
  - o Picture a triangle: God at the top, you and your spouse at the bottom corners. As both of you move closer to God, you also move closer to each other.

So, the **probability** of a strong marriage goes up when:

- You prioritize God

- You engage relationally

- You stay spiritually connected

- You protect time for each other

Hypothesis Testing – IF / THEN in Your Marriage

In statistics, **hypothesis testing** helps you evaluate cause and effect. You create a statement ("If I do X, then Y will happen"), then you test it to see if it holds true.

In the Kingdom of God, we already have a hypothesis that's been tested for centuries:

"Be not deceived; God is not mocked: for whatsoever a man [sows], that shall he also reap." - Galatians 6:7

Let's reframe this in marriage:

- **IF I sow patience, THEN I'll reap peace.**
- **IF I sow affirmation, THEN I'll reap connection.**
- **IF I sow forgiveness, THEN I'll reap freedom.**
- **IF I sow resentment, THEN I'll reap division.**
- **IF I sow time and attention, THEN I'll reap intimacy.**

You can't expect a harvest where you haven't planted anything. The data doesn't lie.

"And let us not be weary in well doing: for in due season we shall reap, if we faint not." - Galatians 6:9

Marriage is a field—and every day you are planting SOMETHING.

Ask yourself:

- What kind of seeds am I sowing?
- What type of harvest do I want?
- What do I need to stop planting?
- What's already growing in my marriage that I need to water and nurture?

Tracking the Data – Emotional and Spiritual Metrics

Smart businesses track key performance indicators (KPIs). Why? Because if you don't measure what matters, you'll drift into dysfunction.

Your marriage should have some spiritual KPIs too.

Try tracking:

- **Prayer consistency (Personal & Together)**
- **Affirmations given this week**
- **Apologies made (and received)**
- **Intentional quality time spent (no screens)**
- **Conflict resolution attempts vs. avoidance**
- **Laughs shared**
- **Service to your spouse (unprompted)**
- **Scripture/devotions together**

You don't have to get overly technical—just **pay attention to your patterns**. Because over time, your patterns become your prophecy.

 Warning: Don't Ignore the Outliers

In statistics, **outliers** are rare, extreme events that don't follow the usual trend—but they still matter.

- One *nasty comment* in a heated moment can leave a scar.
- One *disconnected season* can turn into emotional divorce.
- One *unguarded friendship* outside the marriage can evolve into temptation.

So, while you're measuring the day-to-day, don't ignore the big moments or red flags. **Spot outliers early—and deal with them head-on.**

Spiritual Statistics That Don't Change

Unlike worldly statistics, God's Word is eternal. These truths are always 100% reliable:

- **Love never fails** – 1 Corinthians 13:8

- **A threefold cord is not easily broken** – Ecclesiastes 4:12

- **God is not a man that He should lie** – Numbers 23:19

- **The enemy comes to steal, kill, and destroy—but Jesus came to give abundant life** – John 10:10

You can build your marriage on these **unshakable stats**.

Action Step: Build a "Marriage Metrics Board"

Create a simple board or journal where you track weekly rhythms and indicators of relational health:

- Rate your prayer life (1–10)

- Level of connection (low/medium/high)

- Conflict resolution: avoidant or engaged?

- Date night: Y/N?

- Laughter shared: 1–5 scale

- Unexpected kindness shown: Y/N

You'll start to notice trends—and trends tell a story.

 Summary: Let the Numbers Point You to the Truth

Numbers don't tell the whole story—but they often tell a true story.

If your habits are trending toward disconnection, that's not coincidence—it's cause and effect. But if your faith, humility, forgiveness, and fun are trending upward, you're headed in the right direction.

Let these spiritual statistics be a guide:

- **Pray**

- **Play**

- **Sow good seed**

- **Measure what matters**

- **Adjust the inputs so you get the outcome God desires**

Psalm 90:12 — "So teach us to number our days, that we may apply our hearts unto wisdom."

Your marriage is too valuable to leave to chance.

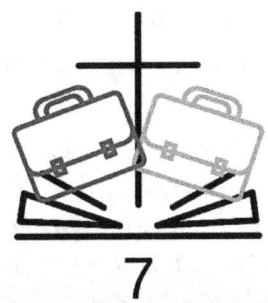

7

Financial Analysis
Money, Honey, & Mission

Money doesn't ruin marriages—**mishandled money, mismatched expectations, and miscommunication about money** do.

One of the top reported causes of divorce is financial tension. Not just the lack of money—but differences in **spending habits, income goals, saving priorities, and financial values**. Money becomes a battleground when two people aren't walking in unity, transparency, or wisdom.

But when handled God's way, money becomes a **tool**, not a trap.

Just like a company needs financial order, a marriage must have financial **unity**.

Luke 14:28 — "For which of you, intending to build a tower, [sits] not down first, and [counts] the cost..."

Financial health in marriage means:

- Transparency with spending

- Shared goals (home, giving, vacations)

- Stewardship, not just survival

Mark 4:19 — The Warning of Wealth

"And the cares of this world, and the deceitfulness of riches, and the lusts of other things entering in, choke the word, and it [becomes] unfruitful." — Mark 4:19

Notice: it's not **riches** themselves that are the problem—but the **deceitfulness of riches**.

Money can promise what only God can provide:

- **Security**

- **Significance**

- **Power**

- **Peace**

If you treat money as a savior, it will become your slave driver. But if you treat money as a **servant to your purpose**, it can build your marriage, family, and future.

Men and Women See Money Differently

In many cases:

- A man's #1 need = **Sex (Respect & Romance)**

- A woman's #1 need = **Security (Emotional & Financial)**

That's not cliché—it's a reflection of God's design. A woman needs to feel **safe and stable** to open her heart. A man needs to feel **valued and wanted** to give his best.

So, brothers—go to school, get skilled, and make money...

Our Pastor always says, "Go to school. Don't be no fool. Make some money, so you can keep your honey." Because when the money's funny, the honey's funny. And ain't nothin' funny about no funny honey. 😊

Translation: Don't put off becoming a provider. It's not about being rich—it's about being **reliable**.

Accounting – Let's Talk Checks and Balances

Every healthy marriage needs a system of **accountability**, not just in love—but in finances.

Ask yourselves:

- Do we know where our money is going?

- Are we both part of the financial decisions?

- Are we aligned on short and long-term goals?

 **Tips:**

- Use a shared budgeting app or spreadsheet.
- Schedule **Monthly Money Meetings** to review and plan.
- Create joint goals. (saving for a home, trip, kid's college, emergency fund, etc.)
- Don't hide purchases or financial struggles—**no secrets**.

"Two are better than one; because they have a good reward for their labor." — Ecclesiastes 4:9

Financial Planning – Dreaming Together, Building Together

Financial planning isn't just about bills—it's about **vision**.

Ask yourselves:

- Where do we want to be in 5, 10, 20 years?
- What's our giving goal?
- What does financial freedom look like for us?

Build a plan that supports your **calling**, not just your comfort.

A Christian financial plan should include:

- **Tithing** (Malachi 3:10 – First fruits)
- **Saving** (Proverbs 21:20 – The wise store up choice food and oil...)
- **Investing** (Matthew 25 – Parable of the talents)

- **Giving** (Acts 20:35 – "It is more blessed to give than to receive.")

- **Spending wisely** (Luke 14:28 – "Count the cost…")

If you aim at nothing, you'll hit it every time. **Plan with purpose.**

Budgeting – Creating Peace, Not Pressure

A budget is not a prison—it's a **roadmap**. It gives your dollars direction.

"The thoughts of the diligent tend only to plenteousness; but of every one that is hasty only to want." — Proverbs 21:5

Marriage budgeting keys:

- Budget TOGETHER (both voices matter)

- Assign every dollar a name (income = planned purpose)

- Leave margin for **fun and rest**

- Cut emotional and impulse spending

- Use cash envelopes for categories that trigger overspending

Budgeting is like date night for your money. If you don't spend intentional time with it, it'll wander off.

What About Debt?

Debt is a form of bondage.

"…The borrower is servant to the lender." – Proverbs 22:7

- Get aggressive about paying off debt.

- Live below your means.

- Celebrate small wins (every credit card paid off is a victory).

- If you need help, consider Financial Peace University or a biblical financial coach.

The Spiritual Side of Money

Money exposes the **heart.**

"Where your treasure is, there will your heart be also." — *Matthew 6:21*

God doesn't mind you having things—but He minds if **things have you**. Keep money in its place:

- Below God

- Below your spouse

- Below your mission

- Below your values

Marital Money Pitfalls to Avoid

1. **Silent Spending** (keeping purchases secret)

2. **Separate Lives** (dividing money, dreams, and direction)

3. **Short-Term Thinking** (neglecting savings/investments)

4. **Selfishness** (spending on self but not sowing into each other)

5. **Financial Comparison** (measuring your marriage by someone else's money)

Build a "Kingdom Financial Culture" in Your Home

Your marriage should reflect God's economy:

- Generosity over greed

- Contentment over comparison
- Stewardship over impulse
- Unity over independence

And most of all—**trust in God** over trust in gold.

"But seek first the kingdom of God, and His righteousness; and all these things shall be added unto you." — Matthew 6:33

 Chapter Challenge: The Marriage Money Audit

Do this exercise together:

1. **List your top 3 financial goals.**
2. **Rate how well you're handling money together (1–10).**
3. **Write out your monthly income and expenses.**
4. **Name one change you can each make this month to strengthen your financial unity.**
5. **Pray together over your finances—invite God to be your CFO (Chief Financial Officer).**

 **Final Word:**

Money will either drive a wedge or drive a mission.

Handle it God's way, and it'll be **fuel** for your calling, not **friction** in your covenant.

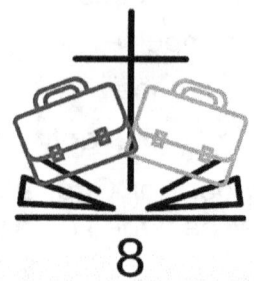

8

Project Management
Building Love on Purpose

Except the Lord build the house, they labor in vain that build it..." — *Psalm 127:1*

Marriage is more than just love and good intentions—it's a **daily project** that requires **planning, collaboration, stewardship,** and **commitment to completion.**

When a couple approaches their relationship like wise builders, they become strategic in maintaining unity, resolving conflict, growing together, and achieving shared goals.

Marriage is **not maintenance**—it's **management**. And good project managers don't wait for things to fall apart before acting—they **plan, monitor, adapt,** and **finish well**.

Marriage is full of projects—raising kids, buying a home, starting ministries, or navigating new seasons.

Never stop dreaming together. What's the next "project" God is calling you to build?

What Is Project Management in Marriage?

Project Management is the intentional discipline of planning, organizing, and stewarding resources—**time, energy, communication, roles, and expectations**—to accomplish shared goals successfully.

In marriage, this means refusing to leave the most important relationship of your life to chance, emotion, or crisis response.

Instead of reacting to problems when they explode, couples who practice project management **lead their marriage with foresight, clarity, and unity**.

Marriage projects include:

- Planning for a baby
- Paying off debt
- Launching a business together

- Resolving ongoing conflict
- Planning a move or major life transition
- Starting a joint ministry or calling
- Managing time and responsibilities better
- Rebuilding emotional and physical intimacy

These aren't random tasks.

They are **missions**—and missions require leadership, alignment, and execution.

Just like in business, projects in marriage fail when:

- Goals are unclear
- Roles are undefined
- Communication breaks down
- Emotions replace strategy
- Follow-through is inconsistent

And just like in business, projects succeed when couples agree on **what matters, how to approach it, and who is responsible for what**.

Managing a Marriage Project: A Real-Life Example

Let's take a common marital project:

Project: Rebuilding Emotional and Physical Intimacy

This is not a single conversation—it's a **multi-phase project** that requires patience, trust, and intentional effort over time.

Here's how wise couples manage it using the concept of **levels of fruit**.

Understanding the Levels of Fruit

In Scripture and in life, fruit grows in stages—and not all fruit is harvested the same way.

1. Low-Hanging Fruit

Quick wins that build momentum

These are simple, accessible actions that don't require deep vulnerability yet—but they restore connection and trust.

In marriage, low-hanging fruit might include:

- Holding hands again
- Daily check-ins ("How was your day—really?")
- Praying together for 5 minutes
- Sitting together without phones
- Offering genuine encouragement
- Apologizing for recent offenses

These steps don't solve everything—but they **signal safety and effort**.

Low-hanging fruit builds confidence.
It says, *"We're moving in the right direction."*

2. Mid-Level Fruit

Intentional effort that requires coordination and consistency

This fruit is higher up the tree—it takes planning, time, and mutual commitment.

In marriage, mid-level fruit might include:

- Scheduling regular date nights
- Addressing unmet emotional needs

- Creating boundaries around work or screens
- Having honest conversations about expectations
- Counseling or mentorship
- Relearning each other's love languages

This phase requires **trust and teamwork**.

Mid-level fruit strengthens the relationship's structure.
It moves you from surface connection to meaningful repair.

 3. High-Level Fruit

Deep, transformational outcomes

This fruit takes the most time, faith, and perseverance—but it produces lasting change.

In marriage, high-level fruit might include:
- Full restoration of trust
- Healing from betrayal or long-term neglect
- Deep emotional vulnerability
- Renewed sexual intimacy
- Shared vision and spiritual unity
- Emotional safety that allows both spouses to thrive

This fruit doesn't come quickly—and it can't be rushed.

High-level fruit is harvested through patience, humility, and obedience to God.

Wisdom in the Order

One of the biggest mistakes couples make is trying to reach for **high-level fruit** without first gathering the low-hanging fruit.

They want:

- Passion without trust
- Healing without honesty
- Unity without alignment
- Results without process

That's not how fruit grows—and it's not how marriages heal.

Do not despise these small beginnings. (Zechariah 4:10)

God often works **incrementally**, not instantly.

Project Management Principles Applied to Marriage

When managing any marriage project, ask:

- **What is our goal?** (Clarity)
- **What fruit is reachable right now?** (Wisdom)
- **What step builds momentum, not pressure?** (Strategy)
- **Who owns what responsibility?** (Roles)
- **How will we measure progress?** (Metrics)
- **Have we prayed together about this?** (Spiritual alignment)

Marriage is not maintenance—it's management.

And good managers:

- Start where they are
- Take what the season allows
- Stay consistent
- Trust the process
- Finish well

Adversity = Opportunity: 9 Steps for Problem-Solving

Let's apply project management to real marital challenges—
because every adversity is actually an opportunity in disguise.

Step 1: Describe the Situation

What's really going on?

Ask:

- What is the current state of our marriage in this area?

- What's working? What's not?

- What are the emotions involved?

- Where might the enemy be attacking?

"Be sober, be vigilant; because your adversary the devil, as a roaring lion, [walks] about, seeking whom he may devour:"—1 Peter 5:8

Marriage Application: Identify if the situation is a conflict, misalignment, miscommunication, unmet expectation, or an external pressure.

Step 2: Frame the Right Problem

Is this even the real issue?

Sometimes we fight about dishes, but the real problem is feeling unseen or unheard.

Ask:

- What are we really fighting about?

- Is this problem worth solving?

- What happens if we don't solve it?

Marriage Application: Be honest and dig deep. Don't solve surface symptoms—**address the root**.

Step 3: Describe the End-State Goals

Where are we trying to go?

Ask:

- What would "success" look like for both of us?

- How do we want to feel at the end of this?

- What are our relational, emotional, or spiritual goals?

Marriage Application: Clarity creates unity. Paint a **shared vision** of what the "win" looks like—peace, agreement, growth, restoration, etc.

Step 4: Identify the Alternatives

What are our options?

Brainstorm without judging:

- What are all the possible ways to address this?

- Have other couples dealt with this successfully? (Benchmarking)

- Are we assuming there's only one way?

Marriage Application: Invite the Holy Spirit into brainstorming. Don't just look for *compromise*—look for *creative, God-inspired solutions*.

Step 5: Evaluate the Alternatives

How do these options measure up to our goals?

Ask:

- Which options help us win together—not just individually?

- Are any options off-limits because they violate our values?

- Which option strengthens our marriage long-term?

Marriage Application: Choose the solution that produces both **results and relationship growth**.

Step 6: Identify and Assess Risks

What could go wrong—or right?

Ask:

- What's the worst that could happen?

- What happens if we do nothing?

- What steps can minimize the risk?

Marriage Application: Be wise but not fearful. Risk is part of love and growth. Identify threats to unity and build safeguards (like boundaries, accountability, or prayer routines).

Step 7: Make the Decision

It's time to choose.

Ask:

- Are we in agreement?

- Have we prayed together about this?

- What does wisdom say?

- Are we both willing to commit to this course?

Marriage Application: Decisions made in unity bring peace. Don't bulldoze or stall. Come to an agreement and **move forward together**.

"Can two walk together except they be agreed?" — Amos 3:3

Step 8: Develop and Implement the Solution

Plan the work. Work the plan.

Ask:

- What steps do we take today, this week, this month?

- Who is responsible for what?

- What support do we need?

Marriage Application: Build in encouragement, check-ins, and flexibility. Honor each other's contributions. Celebrate progress.

Step 9: Evaluate the Results

Did it work? Did it grow us?

Ask:

- Did this solution bring us closer?

- What did we learn?

- What should we adjust moving forward?

Marriage Application: Healthy couples *debrief*, not just *move on*. Reflection is what turns experience into **wisdom**.

Project Management Mindset in Marriage

Here are **project manager traits** that every spouse can grow in:

Trait	Application in Marriage
Clarity	Define the issue clearly—no vagueness or assumptions
Communication	Keep the loop open—talk, listen, confirm
Collaboration	Solve problems *together*, not in isolation
Accountability	Take responsibility—no blame shifting
Flexibility	Be willing to adjust without frustration

Trait	Application in Marriage
Follow-through	Don't just plan—**execute** with consistency
Evaluation	Ask: What can we do better next time?

Jesus: The Ultimate Project Manager

Jesus had a mission.

- He **defined the problem** (sin).
- He **declared the goal** (reconciliation with the Father).
- He **planned the solution** (the cross).
- He **executed it with precision** ("It is finished").
- He left **a system of discipleship and grace** that sustains ongoing success.

Let Christ be the **supervisor** of your marriage projects. With Him, no challenge is impossible.

Chapter Challenge: Project Practice

Choose one "marriage project" or challenge you're currently facing—big or small—and walk through all 9 steps together as a couple.

Examples:

- Rebuilding trust
- Raising children with consistency
- Starting a new habit or health routine
- Launching a shared vision
- Reorganizing finances
- Creating a better date night rhythm

 **Final Word**

Marriage isn't a mystery—it's a mission. It doesn't grow by accident. When you treat your love like a lifelong project with God as the lead architect, you don't just survive the hard times—you **build something beautiful** that lasts.

Strong marriages don't avoid hard projects.
They **manage them wisely**.

When couples learn to identify the right level of fruit for the right season—and commit to harvesting it together—they stop feeling overwhelmed and start experiencing progress.

And with God as the Master Builder, no project is wasted, delayed, or beyond redemption.

"…he which [has] begun a good work in you will perform it until the day of Jesus Christ:" — Philippians 1:6

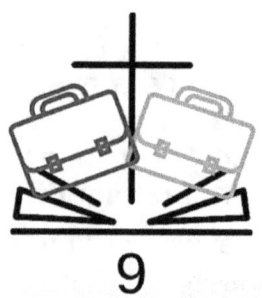

9

Operations Management

Running Marriage with Purpose

"Let all things be done decently and in order." — *1 Corinthians 14:40*

In business, **Operations Management** is the discipline of ensuring the daily activities and systems function in a way that supports long-term goals.

It's about **consistency, efficiency,** and **alignment** between **strategy and execution**.

Marriage is no different.

You can have dreams, prayers, and goals for your marriage—but if your **daily operations** (habits, communication, priorities, attitudes) are out of sync with those goals, you'll feel stuck, misaligned, and frustrated.

What makes a business work day-to-day? Systems. In marriage, these are your **habits**, **rhythms**, and **routines**.

- Do you pray daily?

- Do you communicate beyond logistics?

- Do you set aside time for rest and joy?

Small things done consistently lead to big results over time.

Marriage Metrics: Measuring What Matters

In business, you can't manage what you don't measure.

In marriage, you can't grow what you won't **track**.

That doesn't mean turning your spouse into a project—but it **does** mean being mindful and intentional about the things that matter most.

"Examine yourselves, whether [you are] in the faith; prove your own selves…" — *2 Corinthians 13:5*

Here are some "marriage metrics" worth checking regularly:

Metric	Why It Matters	How to Track It
Prayer time together	A couple that prays together stays together	Daily, even for 5 mins
Intimacy connection (physical/emotional)	Keeps your bond strong and sacred	Weekly check-ins
Words of affirmation	Encouragement feeds love	Track if you've spoken life today
Quality time	Keeps friendship alive	Schedule it intentionally
Conflict resolution speed	Unresolved tension causes division	Rate how quickly peace is restored
Forgiveness	Unforgiveness is a silent killer	Daily inventory
Mutual goals progress	Shared vision builds unity	Monthly progress check
Laughter/fun	Joy is fuel for love	Are we still laughing together?

Three Key Operations: Review – Reflect – Refine

1. Keep an Account (Gratitude + Growth Metrics)

"Bless the Lord, O my soul, and forget not all His benefits:" — Psalm 103:2

In marriage, keep track of how God has blessed you:

- Your answered prayers
- Battles you've overcome together
- Financial provisions

- Moments of unexpected joy

- Growth in each other over the years

Marriage Journal Idea: Create a "Marriage Memory Bank" where you log God's goodness and personal growth. It builds **resilience in hard seasons** and reminds you of His faithfulness.

2. Learn from Mistakes (Mistake Metrics)

"He that [covers] his sins shall not prosper: but [whoever confesses] and [forsakes] them shall have mercy." *— Proverbs 28:13*

Fail stands for **F**irst **A**ttempt **I**n **L**earning.

Instead of hiding from mistakes:

- Acknowledge them

- Learn from them

- Make repairs

- Grow stronger because of them

Think of your mistakes as metrics. They are feedback—not failure. They show you where realignment is needed.

Ask:

- Where did I go off course?

- What triggered me?

- What could I have done differently?

- What will I do next time?

Healthy operations embrace **truth**, not **perfection**.

3. Remember Your Wins (Winning Cycle)

"Let us not be weary in well doing…" *— Galatians 6:9*

A great operations manager celebrates when the system works.

- When you resolve a conflict with grace—celebrate that!

- When you pray instead of argue—mark that as progress!

- When you laugh after a hard day—thank God for joy in your home!

The "Winning Cycle" is the habit of recognizing and reinforcing what works.

Ask:

- What made this week good?

- What did I do that made my spouse feel loved?

- What habit should we keep doing?

Don't forget the good—it keeps your heart full.

Return on Investment (ROI) in Marriage

In business, ROI is about whether your investment is yielding results.

In marriage, ROI means **investing daily** in your spouse and relationship—and watching the dividends of love, peace, joy, and intimacy grow over time.

Marriage Investments	Possible Returns
Intentional time together	Deeper connection
Acts of service	Trust and appreciation
Forgiveness	Emotional safety
Prayer together	Spiritual unity

Marriage Investments	Possible Returns
Respectful communication	More effective teamwork
Touch and intimacy	Renewed romance

Don't just expect great results—**invest in them**.

"Where your treasure is, there will your heart be also." — *Matthew 6:21*

System Alignment: Strategy, People, Behaviors, and Processes

To make marriage "operate" effectively, all systems must be in sync:

- **Strategy** = Your shared vision, values, and spiritual purpose

- **People** = You and your spouse—fully present, accountable, and engaged

- **Behaviors** = Your daily habits and emotional responses

- **Processes** = The routines and rhythms that keep your home and love running smoothly

When these are aligned, marriage flows.

When they're out of alignment, friction and frustration increase.

Monthly Marriage Operations Review (Sample Tool)

Here's a simple review format couples can use together each month:

Operations Check-In Questions:

1. What went well in our marriage this month?
2. Where did we experience tension or disconnection?
3. What habits are helping us most right now?
4. What bad habits or routines need to change?
5. How did we grow spiritually together?
6. What's one thing we're proud of this month?
7. What are we looking forward to next?

 Final Word: Operate in Grace

The most powerful marriage operation isn't strategy—it's **grace**.

Grace keeps you running when emotions are low, mistakes happen, and old habits try to creep back in. Grace restores order when love feels out of rhythm.

Your marriage is not just a relationship—it's a **divinely commissioned operation** with God as the Chief Operating Officer.

"...he which [has] begun a good work in you will perform it until the day of Jesus Christ:" — Philippians 1:6

10

Vision and Order in the Home

"*Lord, allow me to see YOU in every area of life.*"

That prayer has become a guiding light for us: simple, powerful, and grounding.

Because if we can see God in our work, finances, habits—and especially in our **marriage and family**—then we can begin to align **everything** in our lives with His purpose and presence.

But that's a daily challenge.

We're trained to **take care of business** at work. We learn how to climb the corporate ladder, hit deadlines, manage teams, and execute strategy. Yet somehow, many of us never take that same excellence, intentionality, and discipline back into our homes.

Business-Smart, Home-Broke

Most of us have worked for a company or even built one.

And what do companies require to succeed?

- **Vision**
- **Values**
- **Structure**
- **Accountability**
- **Communication**
- **Purposeful leadership**

But when it comes to our **homes and marriages**, many of us run on **feelings**, **impulse**, or **auto-pilot**—until something breaks.

"Let all things be done decently and in order." — *1 Corinthians 14:40*

Yes, this verse speaks about the Church. But guess what?

Your first church is your home.
Your first ministry is not the platform, it's your spouse.
Your first congregation is not the crowd—it's your kids.

If God values order in *His* house, how much more should we value order in **our** house?

The Problem: Priorities Out of Place

We live in a culture where:

- People chase careers but neglect their covenant.

- We grind to afford luxuries but can't afford emotional presence.

- We "keep the lights on" but let love grow cold.

And slowly, but surely, **the home breaks down.**

"He who is slothful in his work is a brother to him who is a great waster." — Proverbs 18:9

Neglect doesn't have to look evil—it often looks like distraction. We can spend so much time "doing good" outside the home, that we fail to **be good** inside it.

A World Turned Upside Down

We're raising families in a world that is increasingly hostile to God's design:

- Marriages dissolve over avoidable conflict.

- The sanctity of life is negotiated instead of protected.

- Parenthood is treated like a product, not a divine gift.

- Cultural definitions shift, but truth remains anchored in the Word.

And yet—there are still men and women **desperate to build families** that honor God.

I *Corporate Marriage:* Kyle & Tomeka Speller I

You are not alone.

But we need to get our **house in order**.

Vision: Your Family's Blueprint

"Where there is no vision, the people perish:..." — *Proverbs 29:18*

This isn't just true for business. **It's life-or-death for your marriage.**

Statistics show that over 70% of companies without clear vision fail. And too many marriages do the same.

So, ask yourself:

- **What's the vision for our marriage?**
- **Where are we going—together?**
- **What do we want our family to be known for?**
- **Are we building a house, or just sharing a mortgage?**

You must begin with **the end in mind**.

When your life is done, and your children sit around telling stories about who you were—what do you want them to say?

Begin With the End in Mind

Picture yourself lying on your deathbed. You've run the race. You've kept the faith. What do you want your legacy to be?

- That you built a beautiful life *with* your spouse—not around them?
- That you pointed your kids to Jesus more than you pointed them to a ball field or bank account?
- That your home was full of laughter, grace, worship, and peace?

| Corporate Marriage: Kyle & Tomeka Speller |

Write that down. Make it plain. *(Habakkuk 2:2)* Then reverse-engineer it into your **daily behaviors**.

Because vision without habits is a fantasy. Vision **with** habits? That's transformation.

Vision Requires Discipline

You don't drift into order. You don't stumble into a strong marriage. You don't wake up one day with godly kids and peace-filled evenings unless you've been **sowing those seeds daily**.

"Through wisdom is an house [built]; and by understanding it is established:" — Proverbs 24:3

Your home needs **strategy** just like your business. It needs:

- Morning prayer rhythms

- Family budgeting systems

- Scheduled connection time (dates, rest, fun)

- Clear values (what do we say *yes* to? what's a *no*?)

- Accountability (what happens when we get off track?)

From Chaos to Clarity: God First, Family Next

God's order isn't complicated:

1. **God first**
2. **Spouse second**
3. **Children third**
4. **Everything else afterward**

When you flip the order—disorder follows. When you **protect the order**, blessing flows.

Legacy Over Lifestyle

Let's be honest—most of what we chase in life has an expiration date. But the legacy you build in your family? **That lives on.**

So don't sacrifice your marriage at the altar of ambition. Don't lose your kids to the glow of your phone or the demands of your goals. Don't miss **the ministry of presence** for the illusion of productivity.

"Except the Lord build the house, they labor in vain that build it:…" — *Psalm 127:1*

Build your house in a way that **heaven would be proud of**.

Vision Check-In (Reflection Questions)

- What is the current *vision statement* for our family?
- Do we have values we live by, or are we just surviving the week?
- Where are we leading our children—morally, emotionally, spiritually?
- How are we modeling love, order, and faith?
- What does "home" feel like to the people who live in it?

 **Final Prayer**

Lord, help me not to win everywhere else and lose at home. Help me to see YOU in my marriage, in my parenting, and in my house. Help me to manage my home like a kingdom assignment—not a side project. Give me a vision that outlives me and a love that never runs dry. In Jesus' name, Amen.

11

"I Love You"
(Four Ways)

Marriage begins with those three powerful words: **"I love you."** But as life happens—kids, bills, conflict, work, change—those words get tested. Their meaning either deepens… or dies.

Let's walk through **four stages of love** many couples' experience. If you're honest, you'll probably recognize them.

1. Infatuation – "I Love You" (The Honeymoon Phase)

In the beginning, love is **easy**. You're drawn to each other. You flirt, you smile, you stay up all night talking. You can't keep your hands off each other.

This stage is sweet—but it's also **deceptive**, because it requires little sacrifice. You're not really loving yet—you're enjoying.

The danger? Believing this feeling is the **definition** of love.

Infatuation isn't a bad thing—it's just not strong enough to build a lifetime on.

2. Question – "I *Think* I Love You?" (Reality Sets In)

Now the honeymoon is over. Bills, misunderstandings, schedules, and in-laws have entered the chat. You start asking:

- Why doesn't he *get* me?

- Why does she always assume the worst?

- Did I marry the right person?

This is the **testing stage**—not of your spouse, but of your **commitment**. Love is no longer just a *feeling*—it's a **choice**.

| *Corporate Marriage:* Kyle & Tomeka Speller |

This is where many couples give up. But those who stay learn that love isn't just attraction… it's action.

3. Conflict – "I Love You, But I'm Mad!" (Real Life Happens)

Real love gets **angry** sometimes. You argue. You disappoint each other. You say the wrong things. You want to walk away.

But this stage is a chance to learn **grace**, **forgiveness**, and **resilience**. It's where couples:

- Learn to fight fair

- Learn that "sorry" is stronger than silence

- Learn that growth requires pruning

You may not *feel* in love in this stage. That's okay. **Feelings are followers.** They follow commitment, effort, and time.

The strongest couples aren't those who never fight. They're the ones who refuse to give up.

4. Agape – "I Love You – Still, Always, Any way." (God's Kind of Love)

This is where the real marriage begins. **Agape** is God's love. It's not driven by attraction, convenience, or feelings. It's driven by **covenant**.

"Love is patient, love is kind, it keeps no record of wrongs…"
- 1 Corinthians 13:4–8

Agape love is:

- Unselfish

- Unshakable

- Unconditional

It says:
"I choose you—even when you frustrate me."
"I choose you—even when life gets hard."

"I choose you—not just because of who you are, but because of who I promised to be."

With a Strong Marriage Plan

Just like in business, **strong marriages are built, not wished into existence**. They require:

- **Vision** – Know where you're headed.

- **Strategy** – Be intentional in love, service, and intimacy.

- **Metrics** – Regularly check in. Are we still aligned? Still connected?

- **Risk Management** – Prepare for storms, and plan for recovery.

- **Adaptability** – Grow with each other. Don't stop evolving.

You wouldn't run a successful business without a plan. Why would you run your **marriage** without one?

 ## The Final Word: Love Is a Journey

You'll say "I love you" a thousand times over your lifetime. Each time it will mean something **deeper**, **stronger**, and **truer**—if you let it.

So, let us encourage you:

Don't just fall in love. Stay in love. Grow in love. Become love. And remember:

- Marriage isn't about winning arguments. It's about winning hearts.

- It's not about being perfect. It's about being present.

- It's not about getting what you want. It's about becoming who God wants.

"We love him, because he first loved us." — *1 John 4:19*

Let God's love be the foundation.
Let grace be the glue.
Let your "I love you" not just be spoken—but **lived**, every day.

Reflection Challenge:

- Where are we right now—Infatuation, Questioning, Conflict, or Agape?

- What's one way I can better express real, God-centered love to my spouse this week?

- Do we have a clear marriage plan? If not, can we create one—together?

 **Closing Prayer**

Father, thank You for the gift of marriage.
Help us to love not just with words, but with action.
Teach us to serve one another with humility, grace, and joy.
Strengthen our covenant. Renew our vision.
May our love be a reflection of Yours—faithful, fearless, and forever.

In Jesus' name, Amen.

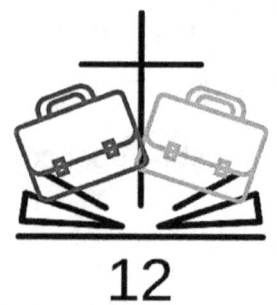

12

TRINERGY
The Power of a Threefold Partnership

"T hough one may be overpowered, two can defend themselves. A cord of three strands is not quickly broken."
— **Ecclesiastes 4:12**

In marriage, strength is not found in independence—it is found in unity. And unity reaches its highest form when **God is at the center**.

A husband and wife can work hard, love sincerely, and still struggle if they attempt to carry the weight of marriage alone. But when God becomes the third cord—woven into decisions, values, communication, and purpose—the marriage gains a resilience that cannot be manufactured by effort alone.

This is not just synergy. This is **Trinergy**.

Understanding Synergy: A Business Principle with Spiritual Roots

The word **synergy** comes from the Greek *sunergos*, meaning *"working together."* It describes a cooperative interaction where the combined effort produces a greater result than individual efforts alone.

In business, synergy explains why:

- Teams outperform individuals
- Departments integrate to reduce waste
- Mergers occur to create competitive advantage
- Strategy aligns people, systems, and resources toward a shared outcome

In simple terms: **2 + 2 = 5**

Synergy creates value—through efficiency, creativity, innovation, and growth.

But here's the limitation: Synergy alone still depends on **human strength**.

Creating Synergy: Business Lessons That Apply to Marriage

In organizations, synergy is intentionally built—not assumed. It requires leadership, structure, and alignment.

How Businesses Create Synergy:

- **Align Goals** – A unified mission everyone works toward
- **Streamline Processes** – Eliminate redundancy, confusion, and wasted effort
- **Integrate Teams** – Leverage different skills, perspectives, and strengths

Marriage works the same way.

When couples drift, it's rarely because love disappeared—it's because alignment did.

Synergy in Marriage: Two Becoming Stronger Together

A **synergistic marriage** is one where spouses intentionally create something together that neither could accomplish alone.

It's not competition—it's collaboration.
Not sameness—it's complement.

In a synergistic marriage:

- One spouse's organization strengthens the other's creativity
- One spouse's vision is stabilized by the other's discipline

- One spouse's emotional intelligence balances the other's decisiveness

This produces growth, fulfillment, and shared achievement.

Key Characteristics of a Synergistic Marriage:

- **Mutual Enhancement** – Strengths cover weaknesses
- **More Than the Sum of Its Parts** – The marriage outperforms the individuals
- **Individual Growth** – Unity without loss of identity
- **Safety and Trust** – Freedom to be vulnerable and creative
- **Complementary Differences** – Differences are leveraged, not weaponized

But even the best synergy has a ceiling. Because humans are limited.

Dynamics: Why Marriages Must Stay Adaptive

In business, *dynamics* describe environments that are constantly changing—requiring adaptability, responsiveness, and resilience.

Marriage is no different.

A **relationship dynamic** is the repeated pattern of interaction between two people:

- How you communicate
- How you handle conflict
- How you express love
- How you respond under pressure

Healthy dynamics are marked by:

- Mutual respect

- Open communication
- Emotional safety
- Trust and accountability

Unhealthy dynamics often repeat destructive cycles:

- Pursue vs. withdraw
- Control vs. resentment
- Silence vs. explosion

Without intervention, dynamics become destiny.

From Synergy to TRINERGY

Here is the conclusion of the whole matter:

Marriage needs more than synergy—it needs Trinergy. Trinergy is synergy **plus God.**

It is the supernatural alignment that occurs when:

- Husband and wife draw closer to God
- God, in turn, draws them closer to each other

Trinergy recognizes that marriage was never designed to be sustained by human effort alone. God is not an accessory to marriage. He is the **power source.**

What Is Trinergy in Marriage?

Trinergy means:

- God sets the vision
- Love sets the posture
- Covenant sets the commitment

It's not just working *with* each other—it's working *with God.*

When Jesus becomes the focal point:

- Pride gives way to humility
- Conflict gives way to wisdom
- Power struggles give way to service
- Love becomes patient, kind, and enduring

Introducing Marriage Trinamics

When Trinergy is present, marriage dynamics evolve into something stronger - **Marriage Trinamics**.

Marriage Trinamics occur when:

- God governs the system
- Love fuels the process
- Grace stabilizes the structure

In Marriage Trinamics:

- Decisions are prayed through, not rushed
- Conflict is refined, not avoided
- Differences are submitted to God, not used as weapons
- Growth becomes inevitable

This is how marriages endure seasons, storms, success, and suffering.

Final Reflection

Synergy can build momentum. But **Trinergy builds legacy**.

A threefold cord is not quickly broken because it is not dependent on one strand carrying the load.

When God is woven into your marriage:

- Strength multiplies
- Unity deepens
- Purpose clarifies
- Love matures

And what you build together becomes stronger than anything you could ever build alone.

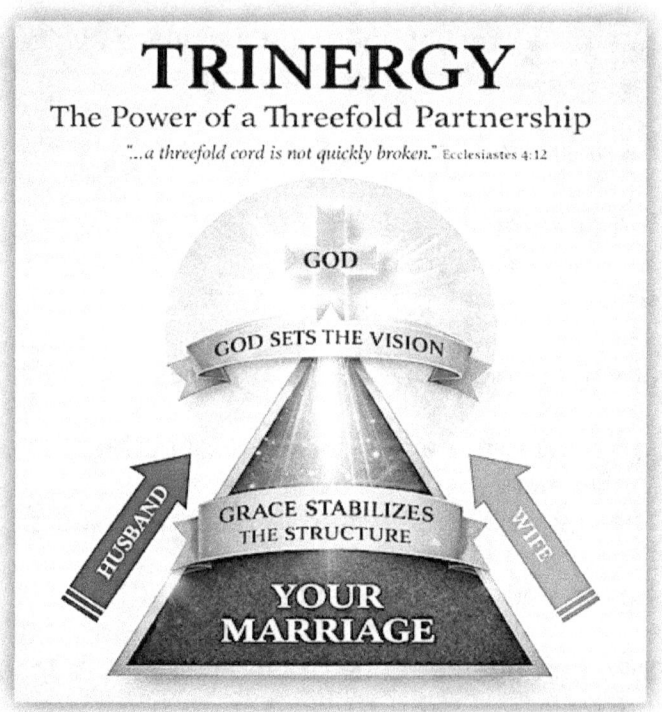

The closer husbands and wives draw near to God, the closer He brings them together.

Closing Prayer

Heavenly Father,

We acknowledge You as the author, architect, and sustainer of our marriages. We confess that apart from You, our best efforts fall short—but with You at the center, nothing is wasted and nothing is broken beyond repair.

Lord, draw our hearts closer to You, and as we move toward You, draw us closer to one another. Align our vision with Yours. Replace self-interest with surrender, pride with humility, and fear with faith. Teach us to listen before we speak, to serve before we demand, and to love as Christ loved the Church.

Jesus, be the focal point of our union. Where there has been strain, bring strength. Where there has been division, bring unity. Where there has been weariness, restore joy. Let Your grace stabilize the structure of our marriage and Your truth govern our decisions.

Holy Spirit, shape our dynamics into holy Trinamics—where our words build, our actions heal, and our partnership reflects Heaven on Earth. Make our marriage a living testimony that a threefold cord, bound by You, is not quickly broken.

We submit our marriage to You today—our past, our present, and our future.

In Jesus' mighty name,
Amen.

I *Corporate Marriage:* Kyle & Tomeka Speller I

Couples Group Study

11-Week 60-Minute Group Sessions Format:
Each couple sets aside time in their personal schedules to read the book/workbook prior to sessions.

Group Size Suggestion: 4–6 couples (*This format can be adjusted by grouping tables of couples & assigning table facilitators to oversee activities 2-5)

Materials: Bibles, copy of Corporate Marriage Book & Workbook (1 per couple), journals/pens

Session Timeline Overview
- Welcome & Prayer – 5 min
- Chapter Activity Reflection – 15 min
- Scripture Connection – 8 min
- Faith & Marriage Growth – 10 min
- Commitment & Prayer Partnership – 15 min
- Closing Prayer – 7 min

1. Welcome & Opening Prayer (5 minutes)

Leader Role:
- Welcome couples and briefly restate the purpose of the group.
- Open with a short prayer inviting God's presence.

[Leader Tip:]
Begin on time and model brevity—this sets the pace for the entire session.

2. Chapter Activity Reflection (15 minutes)

Core Question (Each Couple):
- *Which chapter activity or exercise stood out to you the most this week, and why?*

[Leader Tip:]
Ask couples to limit sharing to 2–3 minutes. Gently move the group forward to ensure everyone participates.

3. Scripture Connection (8 minutes)

Discussion Question:
- *Did you discover any companion Scriptures that supported or expanded on this week's activity or exercise?*

[Leader Tip:]
If Scripture sharing stalls, read one relevant passage aloud to re-center the group on God's Word.

4. Faith & Marriage Growth (10 minutes)

Discussion Question:
- *Did this week's activity or exercise deepen your faith, strengthen your relationship, or grow your understanding of marriage? Explain briefly.*

[Leader Tip:]
Affirm shared growth without pressing couples to disclose more than they're comfortable sharing in a shorter format.

5. Commitment & Prayer Partnership (15 minutes)

A. Commitment (5 minutes)
Each Couple Shares:
- *What is one commitment you are making or continuing as a result of this week's chapter or exercise?*

[Leader Tip:]
Encourage one clear, simple commitment rather than multiple goals.

B. Prayer Partnership (10 minutes)

Instructions:
- Pair with another couple.
- Ask:
  - *How can we pray specifically for your marriage right now?*
- Spend time praying **for the other couple**.

[Leader Tip:]
Give a clear time warning (e.g., "two more minutes") to keep prayer focused and on schedule.

6. Closing Prayer & Sending (7 minutes)
- Regather as a full group.
- Close with a prayer of thanksgiving and blessing over the marriages.

[Leader Tip:]
End with encouragement—remind couples that small, faithful steps produce lasting fruit.

Final Session Add-On (*Optional, additional 10 minutes)
Use during the final week or replace another section.

Reflection Question:
- *After completing this journey, how can you as a couple encourage or support another married couple moving forward?*

[Leader Tip:]
Frame this as an invitation, not an obligation—encouragement can be simple and Spirit-led.

Acknowledgements

To the wisest and most peaceful woman I know—my Beautiful Mother.

Thank you for always being my greatest champion, my steady source of encouragement, and my first living example of grace. You instilled in me a love of reading as far back as I can remember, long before I ever understood what it truly meant to be an author.

I never imagined that I would debut my very first book alongside my life partner. Through your continued prayers and unwavering belief, more books are already in development and will be released in time. When I reflect on our many bookstore visits, rummaging through sales, and the joy of building our personal libraries together, it all makes perfect sense. You didn't simply raise a reader—you shaped the bibliophile I am today.

Rest in glory, Dad. I carry your love with me always.

I love you both, forever and always,
~Tomeka

We extend our deepest gratitude to our Pastor and First Lady for your tireless dedication to your parishioners, including our family. You are extraordinary examples to couples, families, and the entire community. We cannot thank you enough for your constant prayers, loving encouragement to us as a couple, and your unwavering support of our family.

Your life-giving words have carried us through our darkest moments and lifted us even higher during seasons of joy. Thank you for pouring out your personal time, care, and genuine interest over the years. We are forever grateful for your faithfulness and sacrifice, and we pray that you receive special crowns in heaven for all that you have sown into our lives.

With sincere love and appreciation,
~Kyle & Tomeka

For Mike & Rebecca,

Thank you both for the unintentional yet deeply meaningful role you played in inspiring us to move forward with publishing this book. Watching Kyle apply so much of the material during your premarital sessions—and witnessing your raw, genuine response—was a powerful reminder that what God placed on our hearts years ago is still relevant and applicable today.

Thank you for your openness and for allowing God to use us as a small tool in your beautiful relationship. And thank you, Rebecca, for the delicious Mexican dishes along the way—we still talk about them, and we look forward to visiting your restaurant someday :-)

May our Heavenly Father continue to reign over your sacred union.

With heartfelt gratitude,
~XO Kyle & Tomeka

References

Unless otherwise indicated, *Scripture quotations from The Authorized (King James) Version. Rights in the Authorized Version in the United Kingdom are vested in the Crown. Reproduced by permission of the Crown's patentee, Cambridge University Press.*

Chapman, Gary. *The 5 Love Languages: The Secrets to Love that Lasts.* Chicago: Northfield Publishing, 1992

About the Authors

Kyle obtained two Master's Degrees – Business Administration and Strategic Human Resources with Learning and Development Concentration. He is a man deeply devoted to his family, his faith, and his craft. His love for voice work began in college as a campus disk jockey. Over the years, he developed his talent and now works as a professional Public Address Announcer for a pro sports team, with his voice also featured in national commercials and events. Spiritually rooted, Kyle has served as a Youth Pastor, Urban Director, Associate Pastor, and Team Chaplain. His heart for service extends into community outreach and volunteer efforts across Denver. Kyle's greatest joy is spending quality time with his wife and their three children and granddaughter.

Photo by © Tyler Speller

Tomeka holds a Bachelor's in Human Services & Management and a Master's in Marriage and Family Therapy. Also rooted in her Faith, she has worked with individuals and families affected by trauma, domestic violence, and systemic challenges. Tomeka has designed and led support groups & workshops, and her passion for guiding people through life transitions, brings both professional expertise and personal insight to her work.